*WHAT DO YOU SAY TO SOMEONE
IN AN ELEVATOR?*

Also By Angus MacIntyre

Jobs Are Not The Answer... But then What Is?

a book about how to think outside the box using
your gut feelings on social, economic and world issues.

Published by American Business Press
P.O. Box 65624
Salt Lake City, UT 84165

ISBN 1-58982-156-4

www.klog.ca

WHAT DO YOU SAY TO SOMEONE IN AN ELEVATOR?

ANGUS MACINTYRE

Order this book online at www.trafford.com
or email orders@trafford.com

Most Trafford titles are also available at major online book retailers.

Printed in Victoria, BC, Canada.

ISBN: 978-1-4269-1116-3

*Our mission is to efficiently provide the world's finest, most comprehensive book publishing
service, enabling every author to experience success. To find out how to publish your book, your
way, and have it available worldwide, visit us online at www.trafford.com*

Trafford rev. 6/10/2010

www.trafford.com

North America & international
toll-free: 1 888 232 4444 (USA & Canada)
phone: 250 383 6864 ♦ fax: 812 355 4082

Dedication

This book is dedicated to three people who have had a major influence on my life.

To my older brother Lorne who has been a major inspiration for me at every stage of my growth and development. Always a friend and supporter, Lorne has taught me so much about values and ethics, being of service to others, being clear on who you are and living life according to that knowledge.

Mary M. Gillis is the best boss anyone could ever have, a mentor, a colleague, a friend, a challenger, a critique, and a supporter. Mary, although she would not wish to do so, has to share the credit for much of what groups, organizations, and communities have been able to accomplish as a result of my working with them. But she must also, in the eyes of our critics, share some of the blame. I appreciate Mary's feedback on early drafts of this book.

The book is also dedicated to the memory of Creighton Brown, the former Regional Director for the Company of Young Canadians (CYC) in Atlantic Canada.

Creighton was my boss for a couple of years in the CYC and one of the best friends I ever had. He was an excellent training course designer and facilitator for many years with the federal government in the areas of human relations, community development and conflict resolution. Creighton had the uncanny ability to draw out the best in everyone.

He had a wonderful sense of humor and always looked for the funny side of any situation. It was Christmas time when the federal government called the Regional Directors to Ottawa and announced the demise of the CYC. Because of a severe winter storm Creighton had to take the train back to Nova Scotia. In conversation with a young couple on the train, Creighton shared the story of the annihilation of the CYC which he had just experienced. In order to lighten the situation he shared the fact that his other profession was no longer a viable option for him. "Oh, what's your other profession?" "I'm an Anglican priest." "So what's wrong with that? We're both practicing Anglicans." Creighton took a good stiff drink and changed the subject.

Creighton saw his role as questioning and challenging you to think about what you are doing. Once you had considered all the alternatives and made your mind up, he would support you in whatever you had decided to do. A person of high integrity and a great friend to all who knew him, he dedicated his life to making the world a better place for everyone, especially the underdog.

You can read several of his poems – Late Nights and Cheap Wine - on my web site at: www.klog.ca.

Epigraph

"Over 70% of patient error in hospitals could be avoided if communication between nurses could be improved at the change of a shift."

From a recent interview with a nurse on the CBC radio.

"The void created by the failure to communicate is soon filled with poison, drivel, and misrepresentation."

From C. Northcote Parkinson

"The average doctor lets you speak for 18 seconds before interrupting you when he/she has asked you why you are there."

Dr. Brian Goldman – on CBC radio program White Coat – Black Art – Dec. 2009.

Foreward

Have you ever found yourself in an awkward situation, which was not of your making and yet you felt uncomfortable? Why were you uncomfortable if you were not responsible for creating the disconcerting situation in the first place? Maybe more importantly, what, if anything, could you have done to put yourself, and maybe others, at ease?

This book is about such situations and what you might consider doing about them. When mentioning the title of this book to people the response has been universal: "What a great idea for a book." It seems that most people can identify with those awkward moments we all experience in life, whether they are in an elevator or in other circumstances we encounter.

Simply asking people what they would say to someone in an elevator elicits a variety of responses, but seldom silence. It seems that many people can relate to the awkwardness without any description of the particular circumstances. When the question is posed the first thing many people do is to smile. People are also quick to recognize that the principle of what you might say to someone in an elevator might apply to many other disconcerting circumstances in life.

My goal is to share and explore some of these awkward situations with you. In the event that you find the anecdotes interesting enough to try a new behaviour the next time you find yourself in one of these discomforting situations that will be a real bonus. Read on and I hope you enjoy!

Preface

Words are important. Words are terribly important. Words are terribly, terribly important. We talk or write to communicate. It is an essential qualification in our society. Without communication we could hardly exist.

We don't need to be formally educated in order to communicate clearly. As a matter of fact some of the most unclear communications have come from some highly formally educated professionals. Miscommunication costs our economy billions of dollars every year and most of this occurs in the forms we use most often, talking and writing.

Word power is important and a few well spoken or written words can change peoples' lives forever. Just think of Margaret Mead's, the author of Rich Nations and Poor Nations, famous words: "Never doubt that a small group of thoughtful, committed citizens can change the world. Indeed, it is the only thing that ever has." And President John F. Kennedy's words: "Do not ask what your country can do for you, but what you can do for your country." I am sure you can think of dozens of other examples like Martin Luther King Junior's "I have a dream" speech. He talked about his dream from his heart, not a strategic plan from his head.

The reason words are so important is because of the difference we can make in the lives of others with just a few well chosen words. This would seem especially true in those awkward moments in life when we only have a few seconds, or minutes at most, to say or do something that can touch another human being deeply.

It is interesting to note that according to Dr. Howard C. Cutler, in the book "The Art of Happiness – A Handbook for Living" he wrote with his holiness the Dalai Lama, that particular areas of the brain are specifically devoted to the potential for language (page 60). He also goes on to explain that if we are exposed to the correct environmental conditions, that is, **a society that speaks**, then those discreet areas of the brain begin to develop and mature and our capacity for language grows.

According to Kian Dwyer, author of "Living Your Chosen Eulogy" a member of the World Health Organization, it is possible to learn to live with purpose and intention simply by sharing our beliefs, values, talents and skills. What a wonderful thought. To this I would add, we can also share a smile, and our sense of humuor. By doing so, we share a piece of ourselves. After all, is not the most important thing we have to give to others is not a thing at all. What if we thought of our gift as a piece of ourselves?

I find it amazing when working with a group of people in a workshop, laboratory, or seminar how often they have identified "to have fun" as one of their major objectives. This is happening more and more often in the corporate world as well as with community volunteer groups and non-profit organizations. Can we not all "have fun" as we help ourselves and others achieve our objectives? Can we learn how to create opportunities to lighten up or take advantage of these situations when they occur?

This book could have been titled: "Uncomfortable, Embarrassing Moments," or "Awkward Occasions", or "A Guide for the Unbelievably Shy", or "You Can Choose To Be Painfully Politically Correct and Shallow In All Social Situations". This book is not just about what to say to someone in an elevator. Rather it is about those awkward occasions in which we find ourselves at a loss for words. This is particularly difficult when we are in a time bind with only a few minutes, or in some cases a few seconds, to say something or do something to relieve the tension or bring humour to an otherwise awkward situation.

Some people have a natural talent for being "quick on their feet" and seem to be able to come up with the right thing to say in any environment. Those people need not read any further.

By sharing my experience I hope that perhaps you will find something useful for yourself and take from it what you need. I hope that you will choose to become more attuned to those rare times when you can touch another person, even if it is only for a few seconds, and even if that person is a complete stranger. This book is about becoming more adept at recognizing those moments when they occur and taking advantage of them. We can also ask ourselves what we can do to bring some humour to these clumsy moments so as to make them more tolerable, and maybe even, more enjoyable to ourselves and others. We might even arrive at the day when we would not simply be ready to respond to these ungraceful moments but to actually anticipate and look forward to them. I WISH!

Acknowledgements

This book would never have seen the light if it was not for the support, dedication, patience, and editing skills of a very dear friend and colleague, Jaye Castleden from Fanny Bay on northern Vancouver Island, B.C.

Reni Han, from the consulting firm of Martin/Han and Associates in Fredericton, N.B., provided invaluable insight and suggestions about the structure, organization and format of the book. Her sensitivity to cultural nuances and ability to perceive the message from the reader's perspective has greatly increased the likelihood that what I have written is what I mean to convey to the reader.

Finding an artist to provide sketches proved to be quite a challenge. After several false starts, I was most fortunate in not only getting a terrific artist but someone who has a fantastic sense of humor and likes to draw. Born in Brockville, Crystal Covill has a diploma in Graphic Design from Durham College in Ontario. Crystal got her early start in Ajax, Ontario but now lives in Sydney, N.S. where she works for the Sydney River Branch of the CIBC and does creative designs for business, non-profit organizations, window-painting for commercial establishments and art work for friends.

Design and layout was provided by Darcy Campbell from Shot on Site Media.

Contents

CHAPTER ONE

"Perhaps the mission of those who love mankind (humankind) is to make people laugh at the truth, to make truth laugh, because the only truth lies in learning to free ourselves from insane passion for the truth"

— Aristotle

What Do You Say To Someone In An Elevator?

When I have asked someone what they would say to say to someone in an elevator I get a mixed response, depending on the way the question is phrased. For example, if I simply ask what they would say to someone in an elevator I get an entirely different answer than when I ask what should someone (someone else is implied) say to people in an elevator. I deliberately leave this question vague so the person responding can feel free to talk about what they think someone else should say or what they themselves would say under the circumstances.

To personalize the question brings an entirely different dimension to the response. The most frequent responses I get are: "I don't know", or "I haven't thought about it before", or "Nothing", or "Hi", or "I wouldn't say anything, I would be too embarrassed". When I ask why they would be embarrassed because they haven't done or said anything, they often are not sure why, they just are.

But when I ask if someone in an elevator spoke to them would they respond, the answer is invariably "yes", but only if the other person spoke first.

When I ask what you do when you get into an elevator the most common response has been to turn my back to the others and look up at the floor numbers or down at the floor. When I ask why, they say to avoid eye contact with anyone. When I ask why this is important, they think the other people would not want them to make eye contact. When questioned about this assumption they assured me they have never tested this out in reality.

When I have asked people to test this hypothesis the next time they are in an elevator they have consistently reported that not only do other people make eye contact, they frequently seem to enjoy it, especially if it is accompanied by a warm smile. When I inquired if they felt the other person was thinking that they were coming on to them, they did not think so. Of course you would have to judge every situation differently and quickly taking into consideration the age, gender, ethnic origin, and the look of the other people as well as the local culture. But apparently, generally speaking, people do not object to casual eye contact and a smile. It may even brighten an otherwise dull day.

When I was working in the "war on poverty" in Austin, Texas, I accompanied an elderly gentleman in his nineties who was experiencing riding an elevator for the first time. We had to go up twenty plus floors so taking the stairs seemed out of the question. I tried to explain as best I could what the experience was going to be like, but there have been few times when I have ever seen such terror in someone's facial expressions as when the elevator door closed and we began our ascent. All the information in the world would not have changed that sense of sheer anxiety or panic that he felt. I am sure if he had been there alone he would have chosen to walk up the stairs.

I cannot resist the opportunity to tell a story someone told me when I shared this story.

An elderly gentleman was waiting to board an elevator for the first time in his life. He had his grandson with him. He thought they should observe what this new fangled machine would do to them before actually putting their lives in jeopardy. The first time the elevator opened its doors an elderly woman got on. The doors closed and the elevator disappeared. A short time later the elevator returned, the doors opened and a very young attractive lady got off. This happened several times in a period of a few minutes. The elderly gentleman turned to his grandson and said: "Hurry, go get your grandmother, this machine is a miracle machine".

So, for some people elevators can be a terrifying experience. It might be a good idea to remember this the next time we see someone who is not enjoying the experience of being in an elevator. Maybe there is something we can do to relieve their anxiety, even if that is simply to acknowledge how uncomfortable these elevator rides can be if you are not used to them, or even if you are used to them.

Another experience while working with youth gangs in Austin, Texas occurred when I had to re-assign a youth counselor who had been hired just before I arrived to supervise the program. To put it as politely as I can, "he sucked". He simply could not relate to young people and had absolutely no credentials or real interest in counseling young people who had difficulty dealing with authority, rules, discipline, control, and the like. For political reasons I could not fire him, after all he had a law degree and was hired because of politics and was, as they say, "connected." So I reassigned him and took on the counseling job myself. However I had a serious limitation. I had no experience in this area. I had a few courses when I was at Notre Dame University in sociology about youth gangs but did not feel any more qualified than the person I replaced. Nonetheless, I did have an interest in the area and saw the importance of being successful if we were to be of any use or help to these youth facing difficult life situations. You can read more about the work I did there in Chapter 7 of my book "Jobs Are Not The Answer … But Then What Is?" which is available from my website for free downloading: www.klog.ca.

My first challenge was to get some professional help. The University of Texas seemed liked the logical place to start. I knew a priest friend from Notre Dame who was taking his doctorate in Psychology at the University of Texas and asked him who was the best at teaching counseling in that department. Without hesitation he gave me the name but told me to forget about ever getting into his class on Psychotherapy Counseling as it was filled years in advance and he only took twelve students a year. He had been trying to get into it for several years without any hope of ever being successful. I asked if he knew when "the prof" held this class and thanked him for the information. His parting words were "Forget it Angus, it will never happen". The next day I ran into my priest friend on campus and he asked where I was going. I told him I had a three hour appointment with the professor's secretary. "You're wasting your time Angus, he is in class and besides why would you want a three hour meeting with someone who can't possible make that kind of a decision." The secretary made the same comments to me when I made the appointment. Yes, I am sure you are already ahead of me and guessed that two days later when I ran into my priest friend again he was in disbelief and totally shocked to hear I was in the class. The Prof made two exceptions that year. The second was a young architect who had just gone blind because of an industrial accident. The course was fantastic and changed my life, and I hope the lives of others who I have worked with since that time, forever.

A Brief Encounter in an Elevator

The following is an actual example of what happened to someone in an elevator. Annette Goodheart is a psycho-therapist from Texas who works with abused children. She used to live on her own boat, the "Tee-Hee," but that's another story. Annette makes you laugh. You can email her at teehee@teehee.com for a free 10 minute laughter consultation. Leave your phone number, she doesn't type. You can visit her website by goggling Annette Goodheart and learn about her How to Laugh Yourself to Health video. Annette can also teach you about "plerking" a new word to refer to laughter, play and work which open up new and unlimited choices for enjoyment.

In her work with kids who have experienced physical or sexual trauma she has found it useful to employ the services of a huge teddy bear named "Charlie". Because she speaks to groups and organizations around the world she often has occasion to travel with Charlie. Since Charlie is so big (about three feet tall) Annette will usually carry Charlie on her hip as she is going to or from an engagement.

While traveling in Edmonton, Alberta, Canada, Annette was taking Charlie to an appointment on one of the upper floors in a skyscraper. She was alone on the elevator when an elderly gentleman joined her. After a few seconds the gentleman said: "Hey, that's a great teddy bear." To which Annette answered "Yeah". He continued: "that's the best teddy bear I have ever seen". To which Annette responded again: "Yeah". He couldn't contain himself: "That teddy bear is just awesome – my granddaughter would love that teddy bear". To which Annette said: "Yeah – what about you?" The man started laughing and was still laughing when he disappeared down the hall.

Annette has many stories about Charlie. When she bought Charlie she was going to lunch "alone" at a restaurant she had never visited before. She was welcomed with the usual greeting "Are you alone?" A woman "alone" seems to cause a problem for some waitresses. Annette was tempted to point to her teddy bear and answer: "No I am not alone, I am with Charlie."

So she sat down at the table and sat Charlie in a seat next to her. The waitress, without saying a word, set a place for Charlie. When she poured the water she also poured some for Charlie. This drew the attention of other customers. When she brought the menu she gave one to "Charlie" as well. People started to whisper and point to the teddy bear. Charlie became the centre of conversation all around her. Before she left the restaurant Annette had met a dozen new people and received hugs from all the waitresses.

When Annette addresses a conference she will have Charlie circulate throughout the audience receiving hugs from everyone while she gives her talk which is entitled: "How To Laugh Yourself To Health". Sometimes a problem occurs when someone is so amused or taken with Charlie that they do not pass him along. On those occasions Annette has to point to that person to bring them back to reality and remind them to share Charlie with others. Charlie now has received over 10,000 hugs and has made friends everywhere he has traveled.

Wouldn't it be great if we all had a Charlie in our lives? Why not?

Annette also tells the story about attending a professional conference on the nature of humour and she noticed that nobody was laughing. I could immediately imagine the following conversation between the trainer or expert at the conference and someone who was there because they had a good sense of humour, enjoyed a good laugh and wanted to learn more about how to make this happen naturally.

Humourist: If you are interested in being a humourist, then take it seriously and stop acting like an amateur.

Novice: But I don't want to take it seriously. It seems to me that would destroy the essence of what humour is about. Shouldn't it be funny?

Humourist: Then I have no time to waste on you if you think of humour as not being serious. You might as well think of it as a hobby not requiring any commitment of time or effort to make it better.

Novice: But there are lots of hobbies that require a great deal of time and effort. Some people take their hobbies seriously in the sense that they devote their energy and time to improve their skill but not to make it better in competitive sense. And better than what? If you take it too seriously would it not soon lose its joy? I enjoy a good joke, a chuckle at least. I aspire to humour.

Humourist: Then take it seriously.

Novice: But if it is humour it might be hard to take it seriously. If I take humour as seriously as you think it should be taken, I don't think I would enjoy doing it. I am absolutely sure it wouldn't be funny.

Humourist: I don't like the word funny. It is not as professional as humour.

Novice: Do you have any hobbies?

Humourist: No. I don't have time for any serious hobbies.

Novice: But why would you have to take them seriously? Wouldn't that tend to destroy any joy you were having with them?

Humourist: As I said earlier, if you treat my profession as a hobby I have no time for you.

I am impressed with the ads that the Church of Jesus Christ of Latter Day Saints have produced for television promoting one or more aspects of what it means to be truly "Christ-like." The one that impresses me the most is when an elderly woman gets on the elevator and notices an obviously young pregnant woman standing next to her. She looks her in the eye, smiles at her in an understanding way and gently touches her on her stomach while inquiring: "Is this your first?" Although complete strangers within seconds they had an encounter that has touched them both.

When I mentioned the title of this book to a friend recently he told me about a chance encounter his father had on an elevator with a complete stranger. Before they completed their brief journey they had exchanged telephone numbers because of a mutual interest in fishing. They have since become the best of friends and frequently go on extended fishing trips together.

CHAPTER TWO

Examples of Other Situations

These instances of discomfort don't just happen in elevators, they happen in every aspect of our life. All we have to do is recognize these opportunities and take advantage of them.

Church Parking Lot

Just last week when leaving church one of my fellow parishioners, who I did not know, was running to his car. Since it was an overcast day and threatening rain I was not sure if he was running before the rain hit or if he was already late for his next commitment. Nevertheless, I took advantage of the situation and yelled: "Hey, I didn't think the sermon was all that bad". I got a big smile, a hand wave, and a hardy laugh. I am sure the next time I see him in church we will no longer be complete strangers. Judging from the chuckling of others within hearing distance they saw the humor in what I said and seemed to enjoy the exchange as well. I don't know what the priest would have thought of my remark but I suspect he would have laughed as well.

On another occasion as I arrived at the parking lot of our church a half ton truck with a wheel barrel in the back parked next to me. As I passed the truck the driver was getting out. I asked the gentleman if he had the wheel barrel tied with a chain and lock. He looked surprised and said "No, why?" "Well, isn't it obvious," I said, "there are a lot of Catholics around here at this time of the week". He enjoyed the irony and I don't think he thought I was a bigot. He took the remark in the spirit it was offered, a chance to laugh at ourselves.

How it all began

I was not always so outgoing with my remarks or willing to take these kinds of risks, especially with complete strangers or in public. Earlier in my life it did not come to me naturally. I felt I had to work at it. Nevertheless, the first step is to recognize the humour in ourselves. I first became aware of mine in the early 1970's when I was taking one of my first National Training Laboratories (NTL) Institute courses in Bethel, Maine. The course focus was Staff Development: morale, motivation and productivity. The trainer, Brendan Reddy, became one of my best friends.

With one other exception, all of the other participants were representatives from large multi-national corporations, the federal government, academic institutions or Fortune 500 companies from around the world. As a community development worker working at the community level in northern, rural communities in Canada I was very much feeling out of place. It came as a complete surprise towards the end of the program to learn from my colleagues of my ability to see humour in almost any situation. When they gave me this feedback I was unaware of when I may have said something funny so I asked them for instances when this had occurred. I was totally surprised when they recounted example after example of instances during the course when I had made a comment or observation that highlighted some humourous aspect to some everyday occurrence. I was taken aback to learn how seeing humour in everyday happenings occurred to me so naturally. Because of my Scottish cultural up-bringing I am sure that some people would see this as sarcasm rather than humour. I think of sarcasm as a form of humour, even when it is cutting to the bone. Becoming aware of this ability allowed me to easily recognize humourous situations when they occur and to exploit them to the fullest.

A Brief Encounter on a University Campus

A good friend of mine from Newfoundland and Labrador on Canada's east coast has always had this sense of humour. He claims the following story is absolutely "the gospel truth" and happened to him on his first day on campus at Memorial University in St. John's, Newfoundland.

Bert was from one of the many out-ports around the province and had never set foot on a university campus before that day. He headed out across campus looking for the library when he spotted a well dressed gentleman, obviously a professor. As they got within speaking distance of each other Bert said: "Hey, buddy, can you tell me where the library is to?" (It is a common practice in Newfoundland to end a sentence with a preposition.) The professor, with a scornful frown on his face looked down his glasses despairingly at Bert and responded: "My young man - you are in an institution of higher learning. You never end a sentence with a proposition. Now, if you would like to rephrase your question in the proper Queen's English I would be glad to give you directions to the library." To which he immediately without thinking responded: "Sure buddy, I can do that. Can you tell me where the library is to, Asshole?"

Meeting a Stranger in a Tavern

Years later Bert became a field worker for the Extension Department at Memorial University in St. John's Newfoundland. He tells a wonderful story about his first days in the field as an extension worker. After several months on the job in a remote out-port he was summoned to head office in St. John's for his first meeting with fellow field workers. Bert arrived the night before their meetings were to start and went down to one of the sixty-five plus bars or lounges in the heart of the city for a beer.

The bar was quite crowded but an elderly gentleman, seeing his dilemma, invited Bert to join him at his table. Bert obliged and ordered a beer. Then the elderly gentleman made a big mistake. He said to him: "Tell me, me son, what do you do for a livin?" This gave Bert the opening he needed. For the next ten minutes or so Bert told him about his work as a community development worker for the Extension Department at Memorial University. He was working in the out-ports helping fishermen organize into unions, he was "taking on" the general merchants in remote communities who for years had "ripped off" the local people with their questionable practices, he was helping people establish local development associations, he was helping single parent families deal with poverty and injustice, he was ...... Finally he realized that the elderly gentleman hadn't had a chance to get a word in edgewise. So Bert took a breath and a good-sized drink of beer and then asked: "Well buddy, what do you think of that?" The old timer looked him straight in the eye and said: "Well me son; don't feel too bad; you've got a job; and dat's the main ting."

Bert said there were two things that bothered him about the old timer's analysis of his situation. One was the fact that the old timer thought he was complaining about his work rather than bragging about it. The other was that the more Bert thought about it the more he realized how much truth and insight were in the words of the elderly gentleman. The old timer's words have stayed with him and taught him a lesson he has never forgotten.

A Provincial Premier Who Knows How to Treat a Stranger With Respect

This reminds me of another story concerning the Premier of Newfoundland and Labrador and how he treated me, a complete stranger, with respect. Jaye Castleden, who I mentioned in the acknowledgements for helping to edit this book, and her husband, Don, and I have created s simulation exercise about demonstrating how to involve people in a meaningful way in the decision making process. This is especially true when feelings are running high for and against any particular course of action about what should be done. The simulation works no matter what their issue is, whether it is the environment, the economy, jobs, education, training, health or conflict resolution. It could be used to re-invent democracy. You can learn more about it on my website: www.klog.ca.

I emailed all four Atlantic Premiers extending an invitation for them or their representative(s) to an event at Cape Breton University (CBU) demonstrating this innovative exercise. I knew two premiers personally having worked in the same non-profit organization for a short time with one many years ago (his deputy minister of intergovernmental affairs used to work for me in that same organization). The other one I had offered a teaching job before he became active in politics. The other two premiers I did not know personally.

Within 10 minutes I got a return email from a member of Danny William's staff, the Premier of Newfoundland and Labrador, saying the concept sounded interesting and the Premier would have one or two of his cabinet ministers get in touch with me shortly. Within two weeks I heard from two cabinet ministers from Newfoundland and Labrador expressing an interested in the simulation and asking to be kept informed of events. About 10 weeks later I heard from one of the other premiers, who was facing a half dozen issues of disagreement with various special interest groups, with a polite email acknowledging my invitation. Although I did not hear from the other two premiers one province was represented by two senior civil servants at the demonstration at CBU. The dozen people who attended the simulation as observers had high praise for the experience and the 40+ students and faculty who took part in the exercise. In the words of one observer: "It was awesome!"

On the Internet

Of course with today's technology the internet is a potential source for encounters, brief or otherwise. I make the assumption that the vast majority of people either are connected to the internet directly or have easy access to the internet through friends or community centers that offer this service, often without charge. I also try to remember that this is not true for everyone and there are lots of people not comfortable with the internet or computers.

You What, You Quit Your Job!

The next story I would like to share with you appears on my website on the internet. The web site is www.klog.ca. The story is about a brief meeting with my nephew who quit his well paying job that he enjoyed greatly because of a chance discussion we had one night many, many years ago. The incident is described in my first book, Jobs Are Not The Answer ... But Then What is? Chapter One, You What, You Quit Your Job, is on my website. The book is available for free downloading.

The reasons for referring you to my web site are fourfold. First, I want readers of this book to be aware of my earlier work which has a lot to do with thinking outside the box. Second, I want to keep this book as short as possible so people are able to read it in a brief period of time and not get bored in the process. Third, I want to keep this book light and enjoyable and don't want to get too serious about world problems such as employment and the economy. Finally, I want to explore new ways for people to make use of the internet. The idea of referring people to my website and the website of others seems like a logical application of using the internet.

I am always amazed at how many things of significance in our lives happen by accident. This was certainly true recently when I was on a conference call with dozens of other authors from around the USA. I was the only Canadian author on line. The conference call, which lasted about an hour and half, involved three experts sharing with us some techniques about how to become best sellers. However, after the call as I was about to hang up I heard voices inquiring if there were others who remained on line. As it turned out about a dozen of us remained on line to chat about our writings and how we might share our interests and work cooperatively on marketing and the like. We exchanged our websites and email addresses and have stayed in touch since then.

One author was Carolyn K. Long, author of an interesting book called "A Dog's Guide To Training Owners by Shannon the Dog". What an original approach to an old topic, dogs. It is very much in the spirit of this book. As Nancy Peterson, Issues Specialist with The Humane Society of the United States, Washington, DC has said: "A

Dog's Guide to Training Owners is truly a celebration. Its heartfelt message (offered from an obviously enlightened dog's point-of-view) joyously succeeds in 'training' humans to use the most important training tools there are: compassion, fun and good old common sense. A Dog's Guide to Training Owners helps bring out the puppy in all of us and reminds us to live each moment with wonder, each day with awe and each lifetime with love". You can learn more on her website: Prattpublishing.com.

Dog Psychology

Carolyn's book reminds me of a humorous chapter in a book, I Like Green, by a friend of mine and fellow author, Larry Yeo, from Prince Edward Island. It tells a story about five women and a man talking with an instructor about how to handle conflict or embarrassing situations. The gentleman explains the behaviour of his dog and, to the horror of the instructor, how he knows his dog is sophisticated because he only bites people he himself would bite if he was a dog. This can also be viewed on my website at: www.klog.ca.

Occurrences that present themselves for exploration can be found in any number of places, formal or informal, serious or light. The important point is that they present themselves in everyday events, chance meetings or spontaneous events, on the internet or otherwise. It might be unwise to try to create them artificially.

I am sure you can recount events that someone turned from a formal occasion to an informal one in an instant by simply taking advantage of the situation to make a particularly funny or humourous remark. Weddings, funerals, press releases, political speeches, graduations, committee meetings, labour management negotiations, and hundreds of other common daily events all lend themselves to turning a serious occasion into a light one with the right comment. The ironic thing when this happens is how often other people were thinking the same thing but did not risk saying it. Ever had a similar experience?

CHAPTER THREE

What Do You Say to Street People or the Homeless?

The question I ask myself is whether or not casual encounters can be occasions when we can, as Bell Canada says, "reach out and touch someone." How ironic, quoting Bell Canada to heighten our sensitivities towards other human beings. All I know is that it easier to reach out every time I do it.

Street People or the Homeless

When I think about "street people" it makes me think of how strange the English language is and how difficult it must be for people learning English as a second, third, or even fourth language. What I am talking about is how we use a word knowing full well that the way we are using it in no way conveys the exact or usual meaning of the word. Understanding the word as we are using it implies understand the culture of the situation in which it is being used. As a matter of fact it will often mean the exact opposite to its usual meaning. Referring to "street people" is a case in point. We all know that we are not referring to people who literally live on the street. They conduct their daily routine or business of existing on the sidewalk but may in fact reside elsewhere. They may or may not have a home or a regular place of shelter. They may sleep in doorways, in empty or abandoned buildings or in the park.

It would be interesting if someone made a list of such words or phrases that we use to communicate the exact opposite of their usual meaning.

The following is an actual example of a situation that happened to a friend of mine when she went off to university. Both her parents are university English professors and love to play on words. This was more than a few years ago and so in those days she was living in a girl's only house or sorority on campus. When her parents went to visit her on the first long weekend she was away from home the conversation with the "den mother" went something like this.

Den mother: We have a fine sorority here and the 'girls' are never allowed to socialize or visit in any part of the building except here in the public reception area. Any violations of any of the rules or code of conduct calls for immediate disciplinary action. Your daughter will always be safe here.

Parents: Oh don't worry. If you think we are concerned about who our daughter might be sleeping with, we couldn't care less. We don't care if our daughter is "sleeping around" or who our daughter might be "sleeping with".

Den mother: What! I am shocked. I don't believe what I am hearing. You are taking this liberty thing too far. How can you raise your daughter that way?

Parents: But you didn't let us finish."We really don't care who our daughter is "sleeping with." However, we want to know who is going to bed with her and they are not sleeping. Those are the guys we worry about."

How many other words or phrases can you think of that in a certain context or environment mean the exact opposite to their usual or literal meaning?

I find one of the most awkward situations I am faced with occurs when I encounter people on the street who are looking for a donation of some sort. This seems to be especially true if I am in a large city. The best way I have found to deal with my clumsiness on these occasions is to prepare for them beforehand.

What I have found useful is first of all to make a clear choice about whether or not I am going to give anything to someone "begging" on the sidewalk. That used to imply a judgment on my part about why they are begging. Do they really want a coffee, or are they going to use the money for booze or drugs? Are they just too lazy to work? I have had long debates with friends on this topic. The more friends have tried to convince me that it is wrong to give "those people" a handout the more adamant I have become that it is the right thing to do. Their attitude is: "How dare you give a handout to the least deserving of society." Indeed, how dare me not to give to the least deserving in our society and still call myself a Christian. And what makes others think they are the least deserving. Are they not the most deserving? The one thing that is clear is that these people are in need. I have decided that I cannot determine what their motivation

is nor, the more I think about it, should I care. Mostly I have trouble
figuring out my own motivation in any given situation, so how can I
assume to know other peoples' motivation. That is their's and their's
alone to determine and should be none of my business.

What I do is when I know that I am going out in a section of the city
where I am likely to encounter people needing money, I fill my pocket
with "loonies" ($1.00 Canadian coins) or $1.00 bills if I happen to be
in a U.S. city. Yes a whole dollar. I have decided because of inflation
it is not really helpful to give less. When I say I fill my pockets I really
mean that I decide on an amount I am willing to give on that particular
day. For me this means a somewhat modest amount. I consider this
as part of my tithing that is part of my annual charitable contribu-
tions. The guideline I use is to give slightly more than I think I can
afford at the time, in other words, to give until it hurts, at least a little.
However, none of these people give me a tax receipt, although now
that I think of it, I have never asked for one! Someday I will try to
pick someone who I think may have a good sense of humour and
ask them for a tax receipt just to get their reaction.

Having done this I next decide that, generally speaking, since I can't
give to everybody I will only give to people who make direct eye
contact with me. I make a few exceptions, depending on the circumstances, but only a few. In fact this may be terribly unfair because
many of the most deserving people are too embarrassed to make eye

contact with strangers, who are often hostile towards them. But it is a decision that helps me sort out who to respond to and who to try to ignore. When I get close to someone and they indicate a request for some help, often through a sign but sometimes with a simple verbal request or gesture, I initiate a brief exchange.

The interesting thing about this brief exchange is that I am always responded to. (I guess I worked in Newfoundland too long.) I know that many people will think I am completely naive. I never ask why the person wants the money but some people tell me they want the money for a bottle, (and I assume they are not talking about a bottle of water) or occasionally even drugs; while others say it's for food; or shelter. How am I to decide if they are telling the truth? I don't concern myself with this question. When I tell friends about how I deal with "street people" I am often accused of contributing to the delinquency of others. They disagree with me intensely and tell me so in no uncertain terms and that's ok with me.

While shopping in a national department store I was approached by an individual who held out his hand with a fist-full of change in it and asked me if I could spare seventy-five cents so he could buy a bottle of wine. This was not a situation I had prepared for as previously mentioned. I looked him straight in the eye and smiled and he returned the smile. Then I reached in my pocket and pulled out a couple of dollars in loose change. While silently looking back and forth between his hand and mine for about ten seconds I finally said: "you have more money than I have." He looked back and forth and said: "You're right. Do you want some of my money?" He was absolutely serious. I know I could have come away from the encounter financially richer, but in fact came away richer in other ways. I assured him I had more money in my wallet but thanked him for the offer, and we exchanged a chuckle. I then tried to give him the money in my hand but he refused. "No" he said, "I only need seventy-five cents." So I said: "Take what you need." He took seventy-five cents and thanked me sincerely. The next day I saw this same individual with six or seven of his friends standing near a dumpster in the parking lot at the shopping center. They were drinking a bottle of wine. I waved and asked how things were and if he needed any money. He assured me he didn't need anything but thanked me for asking. I later wondered if his friends appreciated his refusal of some money.

But these encounters with the homeless always make me think about important challenges or issues facing us as a society. I recently heard someone in an interview on the CBC to say it cost more economically to ignore the homeless that it does to provide them with housing, health and social services. Apparently two cops in a large American city, on receiving news that one of their homeless "clients" of some 20+ years had died, decided to figure out what it had cost the city to treat him over the years. It was in excess of one million dollars. Interesting? Money can be found to treat the results of homelessness, poverty, poor health, a lack of education – but not the causes. Interesting?

And then there is the related question of whether it is possible to have a society where safe drinking is possible without becoming a problem drinker or an alcoholic. I was thinking of this a couple of weeks ago before I heard the above story and decided to raise this question about drinking responsibility with the Brewers Association of Canada, a lobby group representing all the brewing companies in Canada. I thought they might be interested in exploring this question with me from a research point of view. Would anyone venture a guess if I heard back from them yet?

So this is how I deal with street people. I hope I am not preaching about what you should do. I am just asking you to think about it and make your own decisions. Several years ago I shared my approach with a fellow trainer with National Training Laboratories Institute (NTL Institute) in Virginia, USA. She is also one of my dearest friends. We worked together several times a year in large cities in the USA. She disagreed strongly with my approach. As we walked the busy streets in large cities she would witness my interactions with the homeless of every description on the street. Invariably I would have a brief exchange with each person I gave money to and wished it could have been one hundred times the donation. Although I was not doing much to help change their unfortunate circumstances, I still felt better having made a "human" contact with them. Several years later my friend wrote me an email complaining in a teasing way about the fact she can no longer pass street people without making a contribution, at least to a few of them.

CHAPTER FOUR

What Not to Say and When Not to Say It

An important question to ask ourselves is whether it is ever inappropriate to offer a comment, observation, or a "funny". The common sense answer is the right one. Yes, it certainly can be improper to impose our sense-of-humour on someone else or into a situation that is totally unfitting. It is never justified to say something that is hurtful or may wound, offend or cause pain or grief to another person. So the guideline that seems to work in every situation is - it depends. Judge every occasion quickly, but carefully. What worked in one situation may not be appropriate in another.

This is especially true when we are in a different culture that is not familiar to us and we may or may not know intuitively what is acceptable or not acceptable locally. Notice I said in a different culture, not necessarily in a different country. Cultures can vary greatly even within a province, state or country. You may only go a few miles down the road to encounter another culture. There are no books that I am aware of that can guide you in these circumstances. So beware and assess your environments carefully.

In talking about this book with a relative who is known for his terrific sense of humour, and knowing Larry maybe I should have said his horrific sense of humour, he shared with me something he once did in an elevator. It is not recommended for others and he admits even he went too far on this occasion. Larry was the first person to enter an elevator and it soon filled to over capacity. As the door closed he started to very slowly read out loud the number of people allowed on the elevator and the carrying capacity (usually listed above the door) permitted. Larry said I think there are too many people here and then waited a few seconds and suddenly jumped on the floor. There were several screams by members of both genders. His sense of humour was not appreciated and several people let him know this in no uncertain terms before he exited the elevator.

Another friend of mind recounts entering an elevator with his son Ryan who was two years and five months old at the time. He was on his way to an appointment and Ryan was dressed in his best outfit and was "cute as a button." There was a very large woman on the elevator as they entered and Ryan out of the blue greeted her with: "Lady have you ever tried a diet?" "Yes I certainly have sonny, I've tried them all" she replied while laughing. My friend said he was happy she had a sense of humour and was never so embarrassed in all his life. The next few seconds took forever to pass until he was finally relieved to get off an elevator .

Dealing with People Who Have Special Abilities

This does not mean that you can't take a chance or risk a comment or behaviour that may or may not be appropriate. It simply means thinking about it before acting on it. I can think of an example of this when I thought of saying something to someone on an airplane but chose not to follow through. It involved a person with a physical limitation. A friend of mine who works with people who have physical and mental limitations has made me aware that people who have a serious limitation frequently make up for it by developing special abilities in other areas. When I told others about the circumstance afterwards, "normal people" (whatever that means) were of the unanimous opinion that it would have been most inappropriate for me to say what I was thinking. However, when I told people who had some type of limitation themselves, they were all of the opinion that the comment would in all probability have been taken in the spirit in which it was offered. To a person they felt it would not have been hurtful or harmful to the individual involved. But they did concede that others witnessing the exchange might have been embarrassed, mildly upset or greatly upset by my remark.Therefore, all things considered, they felt it was probably better for me not to have said anything.

For the sake of trying to judge when a remark may or may not be appropriate I think explaining the details of the circumstance I have just shared would be worthwhile.

I was in an airplane at the Toronto airport and already comfortable in my assigned seat while a large crowd of people were still being seated. I forgot to pick up a pillow before sitting and was waiting for others to settle so I could retrieve one at my convenience. One gentleman, about middle age, came through the entrance to economy class where

I was seated. As he did so our eyes connected and he smiled at me. I returned the smile and several times during the next minute or so while he was waiting to move along the aisle we exchanged friendly glances. As he drew nearer I realized that there was something different about him. When he came into full view I could see that he had no arms. When I realized this the thought entered my mind (because of our exchange of smiles) to ask him to lend me a hand and pass me a pillow - and then in the next breath to say – "Oh I'm sorry, I see you have already lent your last hand." My gut feeling tells me that he would have burst out laughing. I think he might even have retrieved the pillow for me since he could have reached one with his teeth from where he was.

When sharing this story with an acquaintance of mine who has a good friend who was born without arms, he tells me that without a doubt she would have appreciated my dilemma and would have taken the request for the pillow in the spirit in which it was offered. He was also confident that she would have valued the opportunity to share a laugh at her expense because people are so sensitive to not upsetting her that they rarely give her the opportunity to laugh at herself. However, since he was interpreting how she might have felt, I will not assume that she would have necessarily felt that way. Sufficient to say I had mixed feelings about not taking the risk at that time.

I recall my first meeting with the blind person I mentioned earlier at the University of Texas because we had a common bond. I asked him if he had a sense of humour and when he said he did I asked if would mind being teased about being blind. On the contrary he assured me. Although he had only been blind a few months he was already finding people feeling awkward about saying the wrong thing to him or fearing not being sensitive to the fact he was blind. He said it was alright if they forgot he is blind because he wouldn't. So we agreed to set up a role play for the first few times in class and in the cafeteria. It would go something like this:

Angus: "Hi Maynard. It's good to see you again."
Maynard: "Hi Angus. I'm sorry I can't return your greeting."
Angus: "Maynard, I'm sorry I didn't mean to be so insensitive."
Maynard: "Angus, relax. Don't be so uptight around me. Be yourself."

As we were parting we would say:

> Angus: "Good seeing you again Maynard. See you later."
> Maynard: "As I said earlier, please forgive me if I can't say likewise."

When I shared these stories with several people with various physical handicaps including blindness, being paralyzed and confined to a wheel chair, or having a limb missing, they have indicated that they would relish the opportunity to laugh at themselves. They express the wish that "normal" people would become more relaxed around them and take a chance on risking their rejection. The feeling is always that they would rather have "normal" people take the chance of offending them than have people simply choose to ignore them because of their own embarrassment. They want to be acknowledged, handicap and all. They do not want to have people pretend they don't exist for fear of offending them by saying the wrong thing.

Friends in an adjacent town tell me there is an individual who uses a wheelchair who periodically visits the local tavern. On a regular basis his friends at the tavern will shout at him as he comes through the door, "Here comes Rory, still paralyzed". (Paralyzed is also a local colloquium for someone who has had too much to drink.) The comment always draws a round of laughter for those present and Rory enjoys the attention.

A very good friend of mine was a highly skilled surgeon in a regional hospital. He became ill with a crippling disease which caused him to lose one foot, then his leg, then the other foot, and eventually the other leg. While preparing for a Christmas celebration with the family he got overly anxious trying to maneuver his wheelchair. He tipped his chair over and broke several of his ribs. His children who had witnessed the accident said he was hysterical with laughter while he was lying on the floor because it was the first natural thing that had happened to him in months. Talk about a good sense of humuor!

Having worked with the staff and Board of Directors of the Employability Partnership (known as Persons with Disabilities Partnership Association) on several occasions I decided to share this conundrum with their Executive Director. She told me the guideline they use is to communicate with people with special abilities as you would communicate with any person you might encounter. In other words, if the situation warrants humour then use it. The decision to use humour is dependent on each interaction. The uniqueness of each person and his or her life experiences will determine the variety of reaction you may receive.

Dealing with Someone from a Different Ethnic Group

A friend of mine from Cape Breton University shared an experience where he faced a similar dilemma. As he was reading a draft of this book he was reminded of a situation he had in one of his classes.

"I was attending a political science class at Cape Breton University (CBU). The topic was Canadian public finance. The professor is the sort of individual who both welcomes and encourages spontaneous participation and dialogue in his classes. Anyway, just how we got on the topic of First Nations' involvement in public finance escapes me now, but another student jumped into the conversation saying he had recently read in the paper where a First Nations band in Ontario was in the process of opening its own bank in the capital city. I was immediately visited by my humour muse, demanding that I join in this discussion by piping up and saying, "Really Gerald, and what will they call this bank, the Tonto Dominion?"

I was known as a frequent user of appropriate humour in class, and this class had no First Nations students who might have been offended, yet at the same time I was offered this 'killer' pun by my muse, I was also inhibited from saying it because of political correctness. I truly agonized for several seconds, and ended up keeping the remark to myself, as the longer I mentally deliberated its appropriateness, the quicker its humour impact dissipated with time. I did relate this to my fellow student in private after class, who roared with laughter. Although I'll never really know if my yielding to political correctness at the expense of what I think was a great pun was right or wrong, I rationalize the event by believing that due to their ages, most of the students in the class wouldn't have got the pun anyway, since most have never heard of the Lone Ranger or his sidekick. Oh, well."

So, did I make the right choice on the airplane? Would I change my decision the next time? I don't know for sure but I think I would do it differently next time. But this I do know. It is important to hear the opinion of people that belong to a particular group whoever they may be, and get some feedback as to how comments might impact them. It is also important to remember that a member of a particular group might get away with saying something which, if someone who is not a member of that group said the same thing, it might be considered quite unacceptable. If I ever see that gentleman from the airplane again I will have a conversation about what happened. I will be most interested in his reaction and what would have been his preference for me to speak or not to say anything at that time. The question you might ask yourself is what would you do in similar circumstances?

CHAPTER 5

What Do You Say to Someone in a Line-up?

A recent experience in a supermarket

Probably the most awkward situation we encounter are those that last for a very brief time. Being in a line-up in a supermarket seems to be one of these occasions.

At our neighborhood co-op supermarket they have a policy to permit various non-profit organizations and clubs to offer the services of their volunteers to bag the groceries as a way to raise money to support their particular cause. This seems to be a very valuable service that is well supported by the co-op membership.

An elderly gentleman was in the position of volunteer "bagger" when he asked me when my grandchildren would be coming for a visit. As is often the case when someone recognizes me and I cannot recall their name or where I know them from, I inquired as to his name and apologized for not recognizing him or being able to put a name to his face. I explained that I often forget a person's name but rarely a face.

The gentleman told me not to apologize because he said that we had never met. "Well then, do we have a mutual friend that I am not aware of?" I asked. "No, not at all," he said. As a matter of fact he had never laid eyes on me before that moment. Then how in heaven's name could he know that I had grandchildren, and better yet, that they were coming to visit me in the next few days. He explained that he simply observed the groceries I was buying. My age, combined with the fact that I was buying lots of pop, chips, bars, candy, popcorn, treats, etc. was a dead give-away. He laughingly explained that his grandkids had come home for a visit a couple of weeks ago and he had purchased exactly the same grocery order. The exchange was appreciated by several others within hearing distance who overheard the discussion.

Potential Embarrassment at Canadian Tire

I am a turtle. For those of you who don't know who or what a turtle is let me briefly explain. The International Association of Turtles is an organization dedicated to raising funds to support charitable causes around the USA and elsewhere. To date we have raised millions of dollars that have gone to support various charitable causes and children's hospitals in particular. It is also a fun organization dedicated to helping us laugh at ourselves and our friends while raising money for good causes.

There is a very strict "code of conduct" for turtles as well as a very exacting protocol for the process by which you become a turtle. One of the first things you have to know about "turtles" is that we never have any bad thoughts; nor say any bad words. In order to be a turtle you have to be pure in mind, thought, and words at all times. Considering these strict rules it is certainly a miracle that I was able to pass the test.

The protocol for becoming a turtle varies considerably from place to place depending on the imagination of those conducting the ceremony. I will not divulge the secrets of the organization in consideration of those who have not yet been initiated. Suffice is to say that my initiation lasted several hours and was most exacting but I eventually passed the strenuous test of intelligence and purity – both of which were a challenge for me. It was also a lot of fun.

However, it is necessary to tell you about the "code of conduct" because failure to adhere to the code can have grave financial ramifications or penalties. When one turtle meets another turtle in public, they are greeted with a special greeting and must respond with the proper phrase, word-for-word, or else pay the financial penalty. The question you are greeted with by another turtle is: "Hey (person's name) are you a turtle?" The way you must respond to this inquiry, no matter where you find yourself in public, is: "Yes, you bet your sweet ass I am." Of course being a turtle the reference to ass is not to one's derriere. A turtle would never even think of someone's rear end. Ass refers to that noble creature that carried Mary to the Inn where there was no room for them.

I was in a line up at a Canadian Tire store when I heard those dreaded words: "Hey Angus, are you a turtle?" coming from a checkout several isles away. It was a fellow turtle whom I had initiated as a turtle just a few weeks prior. I felt embarrassed but without hesitation I yelled back: "You bet your sweet ass I am." We waited for each other after going through the check-out and had a great laugh. I have no idea what others may have thought about the exchange but maybe some enjoyed the obvious amusement we enjoyed. In thinking about it later I realized it was a moment when I felt vulnerable. When trying to figure out why the only conclusion I came to was the fact that others may have judged me as being insensitive to the feelings of people around me in a public situation.

CHAPTER SIX

What Do You Say to Someone in a Waiting Room?

In The Hospital

It's almost more than I can bear
This empty house, when you're not there
The nurses administer their special care
And the doctors have all been made aware
Of my sweetie, it starts to wear
I miss you, I love you,
I said it, so there.

Simon Gillis – Whitney Pier, Cape Breton Island

A Pre-surgery Appointment at the Hospital

Since I am now approaching my late sixties this old body of mine seems to keep breaking down on a more or less regular basis. The doctors seem to think they have to keep reminding me I am no longer a teenager. I often think of saying: "Thanks for that tremendously intelligent insight. I really needed to be reminded of that fact. How many years in medical school did it take for you to become so observant?" I now realize that I am approaching my definition of middle age and will soon be on the downward slope of life. On a quite regular basis, I find myself sitting in waiting rooms in a doctor's office, or in a hospital, or in a medical clinic.

On a recent visit to a regional hospital I was waiting for an appointment to supply pre-surgery information for an upcoming operation. At least on this occasion they only wanted information and not blood or other body fluids. There were two women, whom I judged to be in their forties and apparently strangers to each other, in the waiting room when I arrived. Nobody was talking so I said a polite "hi" as I took my place. We were all sitting close to each other and after several awkward minutes of silence began exchanging the usual niceties about the weather when I offered a comment about the amount of time I seem to be spending in waiting rooms. I shared the fact that I had contracted diabetes about ten years previously and it was beginning to take its' toll on me.

This innocent comment seemed to open the flood gates. The older of the two ladies was due for a breast removal within a few days because of cancer and was very nervous about her up-coming operation. Yet, in spite of her serious situation, she was more concerned for her husband and her family and how it was impacting them than she was for herself. Why am I not surprised she was so "other" focused in her time of need.

It seemed to help when I shared with her that my wife, Julie, had a breast removed some twenty-three years previously because of cancer. The operation was followed by two years of chemotherapy. It turned out to be a uniting factor that brought our four teenage children and us closer together. I told her we had four children in four years. I explained that every time we had sex Julie got pregnant. However, once we figured out what was causing it and cut that out there hasn't been a reoccurrence since. This brought a chuckle from both women. I explained that I am always reluctant to give advice but suggested if I was ever tempted to give in and offer some advice it might sound something like this. I suggested the best thing she could do for her family was to take care of herself as I felt confident that is what her family would want her to do. She agreed. When I think about it, offering advice is nice way for me to tell someone else how to live their life without seemingly to do so.

I also shared with her the fact that many times in difficult circumstances family, friends, or working colleagues will offer to help. Our natural tendency is to assume they are only offering to be polite. So we often accept their offer with a "thanks for the offer and if there is anything I can think of I will let you know," knowing all the time that we have no intention of asking them for help.

When Julie had her operation everyone at the office was anxious to help and when they made their offer for assistance I made the usual "thanks for the offer ..." mentioned above. However, my secretary, an Aboriginal person, knew me only too well. Without mentioning it to me she had canvassed everyone in the office building with an idea she knew would be helpful. She also knew that I would be reluctant to take the offer seriously so she went ahead and organized her plan. She simply gave me no choice in the matter.

She knew I was not famous for my cooking ability having relied almost entirely without exception on Julie for the preparation of meals during our eighteen years of marriage. Although willing to prepare an occasional meal our children were not much better than I at preparing meals on a regular basis. It was a new learning for us to realize how dependent we had become on Julie for every aspect of our lives.

When asked if Julie worked I was always careful to answer: "Not outside the home." Or if the person asking had a few minutes I would tell them she worked but had a terrible working environment and was thinking about quitting. Invariably they would ask what she did. I would continue by saying she often felt she was waiting on the ungrateful, the hours were at least eighteen a day, no days off or holidays, the money was lousy, and she even questioned if the fringe benefits were worth it. In horror they then would ask where she worked. I would reply, "At home. She's a full time mother, housewife, and partner".

So my secretary arranged with different people in our department to take turns at preparing the main meal for the day, including dessert, for a period of one month, including the weekends in order to accommodate all those who wanted to help. We had no choice in the matter. It was arranged. What a service. Nobody could have done more for us. What a gift! The meals were out of this world. Without realizing it I think there was an unconscious competition with people trying to out-do each other. For an entire month, piping hot meals were delivered to our door, every evening, between 4:45 and 5:00 pm. (Boy, what if only I could have thought of an angle to continue this service indefinitely.)

So I asked the woman in the waiting room to think twice before turning down offers of help. People really do want to be helpful.

The other woman had been going through menopause for over two years. She could not understand why her husband had not left her as she described in some detail how miserable she felt she had become to live with. I asked her if she had ever shared with him the fact that she knew she had become very moody and was difficult to be with at times. To my surprise, she had not. I asked if she felt it would help if she did so. She thought it might. She said she was beginning to read about how other women handled their situation.

While not wanting to discourage her, I explained that my wife had been going through menopause for almost twenty years and there didn't seem to be an end in sight. I also said that I thought it was about time a man wrote a book concerning what it is like for men when their wives or significant others go through this stage of their life. The thought of a book on menopause written from a male perspective brought a chuckle from both of them. One of them suggested that if I did write the book to first tell them where I wanted to be buried.

This entire conversation lasted about twenty minutes. I felt I had made two new friends although I didn't even know their names. I hope they felt likewise.

A Diabetic Clinic

Because of my diabetes I have to go to a diabetic clinic on a regular basis. Until recently I was living in a rural area of Cape Breton Island. Our diabetic clinics were held at our County hospital. Although I was in my late fifties when I first started attending these particular clinics everyone else seemed to be older that I was. Not being sure of what I would be facing I was a little nervous the first time I went. So I asked the others what was the routine. They told me I would meet with the dietitian, then the nurse, and then the "team" – which consisted of the dietitian, nurse and doctor. Although this hospital had absolutely excellent doctors, there was consensus among the patients that no one knew as much about diabetes as did the nurse. The doctor always listened carefully to her recommendation before making the decision about treatment.

On my first visit she told me (in front of the group) the story about people coming to the clinic who could not tell her what medications they were taking. They could only tell her the size and colour of the pills they were taking, a situation she found to be totally unacceptable. So she gave me a heads-up that the next clinic she would expect me to tell her exactly what medications I was on, the dosage, why I was taking them, and what, if any, affect I thought they were having. I definitely had the impression she was not telling me this story for my benefit alone but as a reminder to the others.

I settled in for a boring wait. Nothing could have been further from the truth. We were all seated around a large table in a fairly small room, but the tea and coffee were on, someone had brought some sugar free muffins with them, and the atmosphere was very informal.

It turned out everyone came early for their appointments to social-ize. From the time we arrived it might be as long as an hour or sometimes more before we finished all three interviews. However, the time was not wasted. The conversations ranged from politics, to religion, to sex, to world issues, to exchanging non-sugar dessert recipes, to the latest gossip around town, to the "good old days." Nothing nor nobody seemed to escape their keen observations or comments offered with a sense of humour, or on occasion, sarcasm -Rich Little or Bob Newhart would have been proud. After the first session I knew everyone in the waiting room. Without any protocol it seemed everyone returned to the main room after their consulta-tion with the "team", to say good-bye to everyone still waiting for their turn. I always left the sessions wishing they would have lasted longer and already looking forward to the next visit. I was sure the clinic had as much to do with maintaining my mental health than it had to do with my diabetes.

When I moved to a larger urban centered regional hospital, the diabetic clinic appointments were scheduled but I found the atmosphere to be entirely different. We patients are seated in singular chairs along the wall and there is little if any exchange among us. There is no tea pot brewing and no "scones" (a traditional Scottish biscuit) to be had. No stories are being told and generally speaking people avoid eye contact. It would seem to be "more efficient" and "business like" and "individualistic." I can't wait to get out of there.

One of the big complaints in Canada is the amount of time people spend on waiting lists for surgery. But another common complaint is the amount of time spent in waiting rooms in doctor's offices. It is not uncommon for patients to spend hours just waiting to see a doctor, often for less than a ten minute consultation. What if we could create a different environment or atmosphere to make this waiting time more tolerable? What if we could progress to the point where people would come early and stay late after their appointment just because of the atmosphere in the waiting room? Why not?

CHAPTER SEVEN

What Do You Say to Someone at a Wake or Funeral?

When I die I hope friends and relatives will not face the need to say their last goodbye as an obligation. In fact I hope we will all have said our last goodbye long before the wake or funeral.

Twice in my life when I was leaving a job my colleagues knew I would object to the traditional send off. In fact I threatened not to attend if they arranged one. So, on these two occasions, they arranged to have me roasted. Everyone who came had to tell a story about me, preferably one that put me down or made fun of me. For hours people told stories at my expense with barely an ounce of truth in them. We all left the celebration with our sides sore from laughing. What a gift! So what I want to happen at my funeral is to have a simple service and then have people retire to enjoy some good food, drink, fiddle music, and then to roast me for one final time, or maybe not for the last time.

I hate wakes and funerals mostly because I am at a loss for what to say that might be considered as helpful or meaningful by those grieving.

The fact of the matter is there is probably nothing I can say in these circumstances that meet these criteria. The usual condolences "I am sorry for your loss" or "she or he will be greatly missed" seem hollow and empty. The best I seem to be able to manage is a general statement of sorrow for their/our loss, said in as few words as possible, and let it go at that.

I have found it so disheartening to attend wakes that I avoid them at all costs. At wakes one is often faced with the opportunity, or more probably the obligation, to visit with the family and relatives of the deceased for an extended period of time. This can be particularly difficult if we did not know the deceased person well but are attending the wake because we are friends or working colleagues with one of their relatives. This can be equally difficult if we did know the person who died well but do not know much or anything about their family.

I have reconciled myself to avoiding the wake but attending the funeral and a brief visit to the hall or reception afterwards to express these inadequate sentiments to the family or close friends of the deceased. My singular objective here is to get in and out as quickly as possible. Obviously this is not a very good attitude when trying to find the right words to express support for those who are left to grieve.

I was at the funeral of the father of a friend of mine whom I knew from her volunteer work on the Board of Directors of a community development organization. He had passed away after a lengthy illness. I also had worked in the same federal department with her sister for a few years, although we did not interact on a daily or regular basis. But I did not know her father or mother at all. I dreaded the thought of meeting her mother to exchange the usual sentiments of loss when I did not know a great deal about the father nor the type of person he had been. I did know that he was a good family man and had worked hard all his life in the coal mines before he had retired many years ago.

Well for some reason I assume that the onus is on me to say something to put the grieving person at ease. This was certainly not the case in this instance. When I was introduced as a working acquaintance of her two daughters she immediately recounted their stories about working with me. When I tried to turn the conversation to her late husband she accepted my limited knowledge of him but refocused the conversation on me and my working relationship with her daughters. Ten minutes passed like a minute while I became friends with a person who only moments before had been a complete stranger. I did find out a few things about her husband but it wasn't easy because she kept turning the conversation around to me. I certainly gained an appreciation of where her daughters had received their ability to be "other" focused.

One of the things I realized afterwards is that there were few tears at this funeral. It reminded me of what my father used to say when he came home from a wake where the grieving parties were crying uncontrollably for hours at a time. Although he did not object to people feeling a sense a loss and finding relief for their emotions by crying he also felt that when it went on for hours without a break that there was not much faith present.

CHAPTER EIGHT

What Do You Say to Someone When Using Public Transit?

Depending on the length of ride involved when using public transportation systems, I try to take my cues from the people I encounter as to whether or not they are interested in casual conversation, a dialogue or nothing at all. By this I mean I will send out a signal that I am willing to engage in polite conversation if the person sitting next to me is so inclined. If I don't get an immediate positive response I try not to interpret it as a rejection of me but as a sign the person simply wants some quiet time. As a matter of fact occasionally I am in this mood myself when traveling and would prefer to be left alone. I assume that wanting to be left alone when using public transportation would be especially true for celebrities.

A Plane Ride

A number of years ago I was flying from Charlottetown, Prince Edward Island on Canada's east coast, to Halifax, Nova Scotia. It was a small prop plane and there were only a few people on board. I was sitting in a window seat when I noticed John Allen Cameron, a well known international entertainer, recorder, Gaelic singer, Scottish fiddle and guitar player, and song writer, sitting in the window seat on the opposite side of the plane. There was no one in between us. I recognized him immediately. I knew from some mutual friends that he had been in town for an engagement the night before and they had had a wonderful visit with him until the wee hours of the morning after his public performance. My first instinct was to "leave him be" because entertainers of his caliber are constantly being bombarded by the public for autographs, interviews, and just plain attention.

However since I knew we were both fellow "Capers" (both from Cape Breton Island which has a reputation for friendliness) and shared a number of mutual friends that they would be disappointed in me if I at least did not say "hello" to him. So I slipped over next to him, introduced myself briefly, and identified our mutual friends. I then promptly excused myself with an apology for interrupting his quiet time and wished him a relaxing flight. He would not hear of my returning to my seat. For the next forty-five minutes we exchanged stories about our mutual friends, but also about the time we had each spent in a cemetery and what that was like for us. By the time we reached Halifax I had made a new friend.

Oh, did I say cemetery? It must have been a Freudian slip. I meant to say seminary. I often confuse the two words because they have such similar meanings. A cemetery is a place you go to get buried after you die. My superiors in the seminary explained to me a seminary is a place you go to die to the outside world while you are still alive. You can see why I have a tendency to confuse the two.

An Airport Experience to Remember

Sometime ago a friend of mine told me about going to the Halifax airport to meet her sister who was coming home from the USA with her four year old daughter and her new son, only a couple of weeks old. She knew her sister would be swamped with diaper bags, carry-on luggage, toys to keep her daughter busy on the flight, and the like. To her surprise her sister came in sight walking hand-in-hand with her daughter and only carrying a small bag. Next to her was a very tall man carrying her new son and her other carry-on luggage. Since she knew her sister was travelling alone this was obviously a stranger she had met on the flight. She couldn't wait to greet her sister to give her an earful about taking such a chance entrusting a complete stranger to help her with her belongings; especially to trusting a complete stranger with her son. When they got close she realized that the person carrying her new nephew may have been a stranger to her sister a few minute ago but he was surely no stranger to anyone else in the airport. The person was very tall, well over six feet and dressed in black. Yes, you may have guessed it – he was none other than Johnny Cash, who was delighted when his offer to help had been accepted. My friend's desire to chastise her sister disappeared as they spent several minutes with this famous artist who was also such a warm human being.

A Bus Ride

While traveling on a crowded bus ride from Thompson in northern Manitoba to Winnipeg I struck up a conversation with the gentleman seated next to me. It turned out he was at one-time the campaign manager for the Honorable Robert Stanfield, the former Premier of Nova Scotia, when he was running for Prime Minister of Canada as head of the Progressive Conservative Party. All it took to getting him talking was a genuine interest on my part. He had lots of stories about criss-crossing Canada under tremendous time pressures to move from one location to another. Their golden rule was: "Always assume that anything that can go wrong will go wrong."

For every question I asked he had a fascinating story. I asked him if there was ever an occasion when their best laid plans went awry. He instantly recounted one occasion when a potentially embarrassing incident was avoided by some quick thinking on his part. Stanfield was to speak at a noon time rally in a small coal mining town on Cape Breton Island. Bus loads of media were following him wherever he went. My new acquaintance arrived about ten minutes before the rally which was to be held on the second floor above the local credit union. Communications had been mixed up and there were only a dozen people at the rally, a potentially very embarrassing situation. He staged the dozen people present at the top of the stairs with the doors closed while Stanfield spoke over a public address system to an empty room all the while pretending that the room was filled to overcrowding. No one in the media guessed the truth.

A Train Ride

At one time Canada had an excellent railway system for passenger and commercial transportation uniting this country from coast to coast. This is no longer the case. Over the years I had often used the rail system as the most desirable of my public transportation choices. Because of special circumstances there was a period of several months when I took the train from Halifax to Sydney, N.S. every second weekend. I was working for the national park service, Parks Canada as a consultant on how to involve the public in a meaningful way in the preparation of management plans for several of their national parks in Atlantic Canada. At the same time I was completing my Masters Degree in Adult Education from St. F.X. University in Antigonish, N.S. I used the twelve hour train ride to write my master's thesis.

Most of the time on these trips people would see me engrossed in piles of papers and, to my delight, decide to ignore me. Occasionally I would take a break from the task at hand and would invariably end up in an interesting conversation with a complete stranger. As indicated earlier, the trick of a good conversation is to remain "other focused" and not let the exchange revert back to oneself.

A Ferry Ride

For several years in the late 1960's I worked on Prince Edward Island on the east coast of Canada. The only access to the Island was by air or several car/passenger ferries so I often had occasion to make the crossing by ferry. The crossings generally took just over an hour. Passengers were expected to vacate their vehicles and go to an upper deck where dining and washrooms were available. On one occasion the dining room was very crowded and I invited an elderly couple to join me at my table. During the course of the conversation we got talking about famous "Islanders." One of the people I mentioned was Stompin' Tom Connors, an internationally recognized Canadian folk singer of great fame. Suddenly the couple whispered. "Stompin' Tom was not an Islander." "What," I said. "Stompin' Tom not an Islander, why that's heresy. Everybody knows Stompin' Tom is from West Prince, PEI. I have friends who know him well and have even visited his home in Skinner's Pond." "No," they repeated as they continued to whisper, "He was actually three months old when he came to PEI from New Brunswick." I am sure we all know of communities where if you were not born there you will never really belong.

I found a way to get around this problem on more than one occasion. I mentioned in the preface the importance of words. I worked on P.E.I. for over three years. During that time I was frequently asked if I was "an Islander" to which I always responded yes. The last name MacIntyre was not an uncommon name on **thee** Island. I was born on Cape Breton Island. I knew that people asking were referring to P.E.I. Only occasionally did someone ask me what part of the Island I was from. When I responded that my home town was Sydney (on the nearby Island of Cape Breton) they informed me that Cape Breton Island was not "**thee**" Island. I responded, Cape Breton certainly was "thee" Island if you are from there. They laughed and said they hadn't thought of it that way.

On another occasion while crossing to PEI I was on the newest ferry. The federal government had just built two new ferries for the crossing and had commissioned them "Holiday Island" and "Vacation Land". I was talking with one of the crew about the new ferries and asked what people thought of them. He said "Islanders" really like everything about them except their names. I asked what they thought they should be called. He immediately answered the "Fuddle" and the "Duddle." A few months previous our Prime Minister at the time, Pierre Trudeau, was asked what he thought of a particular situation. According to the media he had responded by using the "f" word a couple of times. He later claimed that what he said was "Fuddle Duddle."

I have often had similar experiences when working travelling back and forth on the ferry to Newfoundland. The province of Newfoundland and Labrador joined Canada in 1949 with a " landslide" vote of fifty-one per cent of the population. Not surprisingly some Newfoundlanders still feel they have never been given their "just due" by "mainlanders," a not so endearing term they often use to refer to other Canadians. Having lived in several parts of the USA I know that there are southerners and members of minority groups throughout the country who can relate to these feelings of disconnectedness and isolation.

Jokes about Newfoundlanders are as prominent in Canada as Polish jokes are elsewhere. But one Newfoundland joke that local people like to share is: "What is black and blue and floats all over?" The answer is the next mainlander that tells a Newfoundland joke. It seems like many nationalities have to have someone else to put down in order to feel better about themselves.

People would ask me, not if I am from Newfoundland and Labrador, but: "Are you a mainlander?" To which I generally replied: "No I am not. But I am not from "the Rock" (a term of affection for Newfoundland) either, I am a Cape Bretoner." Cape Bretoners, Newfoundlanders and Labradorians are often equally looked down upon by the rest of Canada. So being from "the Cape" one is considered to be one of the Newfoundland family – just a slightly distant cousin!

An Unbelievable Taxi Ride

I was in San Francisco delivering a nine day laboratory training program for senior executives representing international companies around the world. Mid way through the program we had a mid-program break. The other trainer and I called a cab and headed for the famous San Francisco "fisherman's wharf" area. Since it was our first trip to San Francisco we were anxious to see as much of the city as we could during our time off. When the cab driver, a rather talkative fellow, found out we were from Cape Breton Island in Canada he almost went ballistic. He had visited Cape Breton Island many years ago while on vacation and felt he had never before or since experienced such hospitality and genuine friendliness. Complete strangers invited him onto their fishing boats and to stay with them rather than in a commercial establishment. He turned off the meter, reported off for the rest of the afternoon and showed us all the sights that you could hope to see in one afternoon. It was a real battle getting him to allow us to treat him to a nice supper. What an unforgettable experience with someone who only a few hours earlier had been a complete stranger to us.

CHAPTER NINE

What to Say to Someone in a Public Washroom

This chapter might have been titled what to say to someone before, during, or after using a public washroom.

One before story is about my friend Creighton Brown who is one of the people this book is dedicated to. As mentioned in the dedication Creighton was an Anglican priest, my boss in the Company of Young Canadians, and someone with a terrific sense of humour. One day when he was visiting me in Sydney we went out to lunch with several of our volunteers. Creighton often reminded them they were called volunteer CYC youth workers because we paid them so poorly. On this occasion when he came back from the washroom our very young waitress asked us how things were and Creighton said the meal was great but he had a complaint about the bubble gum machines in the washroom. When he realized she didn't know what he was talking about Creighton complained about the fact the gum was just like rubber and had an awful taste to it. She offered to tell the manager but Creighton assured her it was not that big a deal – at least not in his case. I'm sure she didn't know what was so funny about the stupid gum machine.

The friend of mine who suggested this chapter because she finds washroom situations uncomfortable says she will often say to a friend who has come back from using a public washroom: "Well that didn't take long, are you sure you washed your hands?" Most people take it in the spirit it was offered and laugh about it.

Another friend of mine who was Aboriginal and had a terrific sense of humour told me the story about combing his hair before proceeding to wash his hands after using the washroom. A non-Native standing next to him couldn't wait to put him down and asked if his father ever taught him to wash his hands after using the urinal. "No," he quickly replied, "unlike your father he taught me not to pee all over my hands when I use the bathroom."

A relative of mine has a standing comment when he gets up to go to the washroom. "I think I'll go to the washroom before I forget." It always brings a chuckle.

There is no doubt that washroom situations have the potential to be awkward is not outright embarrassing. This is one situation where I think there might be a real gender difference in how it is experienced. For one thing women will often go to the washroom in two's or even in small groups. It makes one wonder if in fact it is as much a social situation as it is a physical need that is being met. They certainly seem to enjoy the experience more than men. They often come back with the hint that lots of important things were talked about but in the complete confidentiality of "washroom etiquette" which will never be broken. I think this is because women, generally speaking, tend to be more process oriented which means they are more interested in experiencing and enjoying the moment and engaging the other person rather than being concerned about the eventual outcome of the conversation. This is why they are more likely to look you straight in the eye when talking with you even if they are talking about a mundane topic like what dressing they used to top off the salad at last night's supper.

Meeting strangers in a washroom can be awkward. Standing next to people in a crowded toilet where every urinal is in use makes staring straight ahead mandatory. However one thoughtful public washroom attendant at an Irving service station has reduce the clumsiness of this moment by placing the latest copy of different pages from the Globe and Mail national newspaper on the wall in front of each stall.

Have you even thought about why urinals never face each other in a men's washroom? I think one answer is because men would be so embarrassed they wouldn't be able to go. Have you ever found someone using a urinal looking at the person next to them and carrying on a conversation? I might happen occasionally but not very often.

CHAPTER TEN

What Do You Say to Someone When Surrounded by Hundreds or Thousands?

One of the things you can assume if you go to a huge public event is that most of the people there are like-minded. That is to say if it is a sporting event then chances are pretty good they are there because they enjoy that particular sport. If you are in an ice arena then the people there enjoy hockey or figure skating or some other ice sport.

On one such occasion a friend of mind, Donnie MacPhee, went to the arena to see the local hockey team take on a team from the Port Hood area, the other side of Cape Breton Island. The usual protocol at such events is for players supporting a particular team usually sat on the same side of the rink behind their "bench" and were quite loud in support of their team. On this occasion Donnie experienced two rather boisterous young ladies supporting the opposition sitting next to him on the wrong side of the rink. Actually they were yelling support for their boyfriends who played for "the good guys." This was unusual for opponents to venture into the camp of "the enemy" and so he inquired where they were from. One responded: "Oh you wouldn't know the place, nobody in the industrial area ever heard of it. "Well", Donnie said, "try me because I know the Island fairly well." "We're from a little place called rear Creignish, near Judique." To which Donnie responded "You look a lot like one of John Duncan's daughters. How is John Duncan these days?" The girl was shocked. It turns out she was one of JD's kids, in fact a cousins he had not seen in many years.

That reminds me of the story that was told to me as "the gospel truth" (you know you are going to hear a real whopper when you hear that phrase) about the fellow "from away" who came to Centre 200 over the holidays because he had heard that an occasional hockey game broke out in the middle of the fights at the local arena. He noticed that one person had an empty seat next to him which had not been filled part way through the first period. He couldn't resist the temptation to get a better view of the game and finally asked the fellow if the seat next to him was going to be occupied. The elderly gentleman said no and invited him to join him. During the intermission, after the exchange of several hockey stories, he inquired as to why the seat was empty. "Oh," he said, "My wife and I have had season tickets for over twenty-five years and she passed away recently." "I'm so sorry to hear that, but don't you have any friends or relatives who would love to accompany you to a game?" " I certainly do," replied the gentleman, "but they are all at her wake."

If you are at a folk concert then there is a good chance the audience is into folk music or at least the music of the particular artist that is being featured at that concert. So, even in a crowd of hundreds or thousands, we can have a shared interest or experience.

Be Careful, You Never Know Who You Are Talking To

Every fall for an extended period there is an international gathering on Cape Breton Island called the Celtic Colors. According to a tourist magazine after Hawaii Cape Breton Island is the number two island destination in the world for North American tourists. Celtic Colors is now the number one tourist attraction in Canada. It is held in the fall because the mountains and hills on the Island come alive with the most beautiful colors imaginable. In the words of Alexander Graham Bell "I have traveled extensively, seen the seven wonders of the world, been to the Alps and Rocky mountains but for sheer beauty Cape Breton outrivals them all."

One of the things visitors to Cape Breton Island are warned about is to be careful about making negative remarks about anyone; you never know who you are talking to. Last fall I was attending a Celtic Colors Scottish piano event at our local university. During intermission I struck up a conversation with the gentleman sitting next to me. He was from the Midwest in the USA and every few years scheduled his trip to visit a cousin during the Celtic Colors. His cousin was a professor at Cape Breton University (CBU). I mentioned that I occasionally taught at CBU. He told me the professor's name was, Dr. Gertrude MacIntyre, and inquired if by any chance I knew her. After several moments of careful consideration I said that I thought I might indeed know her – she was my sister-in-law!

CHAPTER ELEVEN

Can We Create Situations for Meaningful Exchanges If We Only Have a Brief Moment for Interaction?

The simply answer to this question is "not easily." As mentioned in chapter two, it might be unwise to try and create these artificially. It is difficult if not impossible to create a spontaneous response to an artificial situation which we have created ourselves. However, being ready for them can help.

What seems appropriate is simply to think about circumstances in everyday life which potentially lend themselves to embarrassing or awkward moments. If we have given this possibility some previous thought then, when these events occur, we can be better prepared to take advantage of them.

It was Christmas week and there was a long line when I had placed and paid for my order at the local Dairy Queen. I was standing adjacent to the line-up waiting for my order to be filled. The next person in line, a young lady, had placed her order and the clerk, an elderly gentleman, announced: "that will be $12.99." She gave him $13.00 and I couldn't resist the opportunity to say: "What the hell, it's Christmas week, tell him to keep the change." Both of them burst out laughing as did several others in the line-up who heard the exchange. We all exchanged smiles. It was taken in the spirit in which it was offered – a chance to laugh at ourselves.

CHAPTER TWELVE

Go For It and Enjoy!

So, do I have an answer for what to say to someone in an elevator? Yes, and it is guaranteed to work in any situation. The answer is – it depends. For those who will not find this helpful the answer is 42.

Another option is to enter a crowded elevator and remain facing everyone. When the elevator doors have closed announce: "You are probably wondering why I called this meeting on such short notice. Well, the world is in a mess and it's up to us to correct the problem. We should meet again in one year to report on our progress in making the world a better place. Thanks for coming and enjoy the day." I tried this on a couple of occasions and received a warm response each time.

But we can only answer this question for ourselves. I hope this book has been helpful in assisting you to think about those awkward moments we all experience in life. Will you risk new behavior with the hope that you may lighten someone else's load in what has, for all too often, for all too many, become a very burdensome life? I hope so.

I encourage you to take a risk, share yourself, and enjoy even those awkward moments. You might be pleasantly surprised at the results.

Finally my serenity prayer for all my readers:

"May God grant you the senility to forget the people you never liked anyway, the good fortune to run into the ones you do, and the eyesight to tell the difference."

"Be happy!"

About the Author

With the exception of the time spent (after dropping out of high school) as a delivery salesman (grocery, milk and ice cream truck driver) and his year as a laborer at the Sydney Steel Plant (after five years in university), Angus spent his working life being employed at the community level in community development; organizational development (especially with nonprofit organizations); community-based economic development; education; and designing and conducting leadership training for civil servants, academics, business people and community leaders. Angus was active in the anti-war and civil-rights movements in the early sixties in the U.S., including the organization of Home Educational Visits—a movement begun in Chicago to encourage dialogue and over time hopefully change attitudes of the majority toward the minorities. He once spent forty-eight days on a vigil in front of the Lincoln Memorial in Washington, D.C., until the civil-rights legislation passed in 1964. Angus has worked on the war on poverty in Texas; as a Public Participation Officer for a special NATO project in Canada; with First Nations across Canada including the Northwest Territories, northern Manitoba and northern Ontario, New Brunswick, Nova Scotia, Prince Edward Island, and Labrador. He intentionally changed jobs every three or four years and sometimes even more often.

Angus earned his BA degree from Notre Dame University in South Bend, Indiana; did postgraduate work at Holy Cross College in Washington, D.C., the University of Michigan, the University of Texas and California State University; and obtained his master's degree in adult education from St. Francis Xavier University in Nova Scotia.

For over fifteen years, Angus was a professional member of the National Training Laboratories (NTL) Institute for Applied Behavioral Science in Virginia, where he taught senior executives from multi-national corporations several programs including Human Interaction, Team Building, Complex Systems Change and Management Work Conferences for senior managers. He holds a professional designation as an economic developer (Ec.D.) from the University of Waterloo and the Economic Development Association of Canada (EDAC). Angus is a Certified Human Resource Professional (CHRP) as well as a certified Program Leader for Kepner Tregoe's Planning, Problem Solving, and Decision Making.